THE IMPACT & PRESENCE POCKETBOOK

By Pam Jones & Janie van Hool

Drawings by Phil Hailstone

"This little gem tells you all you need to know about making a positive impact. The user-friendly format and excellent content make it essential for anyone in business."
Maura O'Mahony, Management Development Manager, Allied Irish Bank (GB)

"Provides invaluable advice on how to develop yourself, great tips and hints on how to do it and useful exercises to get you started."
James Moncrieff, Director, LMT Consulting

"A fun, pragmatic approach developed by experts in their fields. Applicable in areas of business and personal life."
Monica Kinder, Assistant Manager, Management Development, Allied Irish Bank (GB)

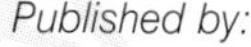
Published by:
Management Pocketbooks Ltd
Laurel House, Station Approach, Alresford, Hants SO24 9JH, U.K.
Tel: +44 (0)1962 735573   Fax: +44 (0)1962 733637
E-mail: sales@pocketbook.co.uk
Website: www.pocketbook.co.uk

This edition published 2004.

British Library Cataloguing-in-Publication Data – A catalogue record for this book is available from the British Library.

ISBN 1 903776 18 X

Design, typesetting and graphics by **efex ltd**. Printed in U.K.

CONTENTS

4

INTRODUCTION

WHO SHOULD USE THIS BOOK?

This book is for people in business who want to maximise their presence and create a powerful impact on the people they meet and work with. It provides a wealth of tips and techniques, using questionnaires and exercises to help you assess your impact, and enhance your communication style and strategy.

The book shows you how to appear confident and use a dynamic style of communication, but also how to feel positive and self-assured in any situation. It takes a holistic approach, helping you to project an image that reflects your values and strengths.

The authors bring together experience from the worlds of business and theatre to provide a broad perspective on the benefits of taking control of personal impact.

IS THIS BOOK FOR YOU?

- Do you want to make the most of yourself?
- Do you think you could make greater impact?
- Do you need to prepare yourself for a meeting or interview?
- Do you want to create an image which reflects your abilities?
- Do you want to enhance your leadership capability?

If so read on.

'You never know when you are making a memory.'
Rickie Lee-Jones

INTRODUCTION

IMPACT AND PRESENCE – WHY SO IMPORTANT?

'It takes 30 seconds to make an impact.'
Albert Mehrabian, Silent Messages, Wadsworth, 1971, 1985

Your image and how you use it is central to others' perception of your abilities, skills and potential. It is amazing how quickly you make an impression on others.

You need to pay attention to your image because:

- To develop your career you will need to sell yourself to others
- In a service economy people buy ***you***
- While adapting to the environment you work in you need to stay true to yourself, and know how to do this
- There is a clear relationship between impact and self-concept; each feeds off the other
- Confidence is contagious, but so is lack of confidence
- You have the ability to create the atmosphere you work in through generating a positive impact

Projecting the right image can mean the difference between success and failure.

WHAT IS IMPACT AND PRESENCE?

We are so much more than what we do.

Career progression is not just about doing a good job, but about:

- Getting exposure with key people
- Visibility
- Personal credibility
- Networking
- Sending out the right messages
- Being positive
- Creating the right image

Your personal presence is the experience people have of you and the memory of you they will take away.

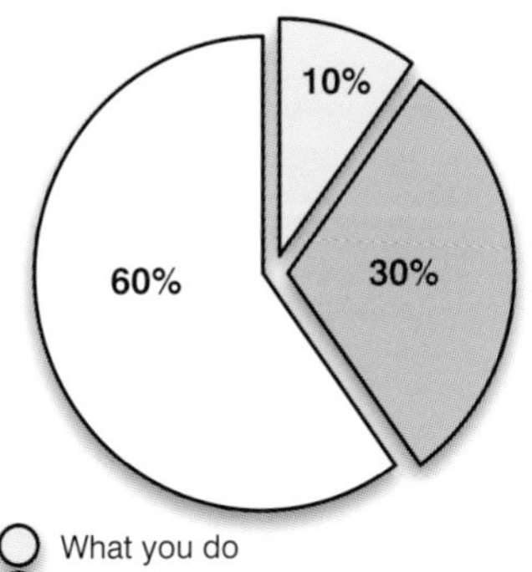

INTRODUCTION

WHO MAKES IMPACT AND HOW?

In the media every day we are bombarded with images of people who make an impact: politicians (nationally and internationally), actors, artists, sporting heroes, etc. These people inspire strong reactions from their audience, both positive and negative.

Before you can effectively make an impact, or make yourself memorable to the audience that you face (be that one person or a thousand), you need to have a clear idea of what you think impact is, or should be, to give you the results you want.

Think of some famous people that you would define as being charismatic, having personal presence, creating impact, and try to define what it is about them that gives them this quality.

Chances are, you'll have focused on people whose image is everywhere, but who are unknown to you, other than in pictures or on TV.

Now try the exercise with people you know, or have met. Analyse what it is that they think, feel, say and do that gives them this quality and then define which of those qualities you share with them or would like to develop.

START RIGHT NOW

To create impact you need to work on yourself in a number of different ways. Using this book, you can work systematically through each section or dip in at the appropriate place.

Gaining control – the inner thinking toolkit	• Understanding yourself • Being mentally prepared • Getting support
Impact from the outside in	• Communicating with impact • Creating physical presence • Using your voice
Developing your personal brand	• Identifying your brand • Creating your brand • Developing brand awareness
Adapting to the environment	• Adapting your style • Creating impact in different situations • Planning for success

START RIGHT NOW

Inner thinking toolkit

Impact from the outside in

Developing your personal brand

Adapting to the environment

GAINING CONTROL - THE INNER THINKING TOOLKIT

QUESTIONNAIRE

Impact and presence is as much about **YOU** as it is about how you look. This section will focus on your 'inner engine'. Look at the questions below to determine how aware you are of the importance of your inner thinking toolkit. Spend some time reflecting on your answers.

Each question relates to some aspect of your self-confidence and how this is expressed.

1	Do you think positively or negatively about your impact on others?
2	When communicating, do you ever anticipate what others might be thinking about you?
3	How does stress manifest itself with you?
4	Do you control your stress levels when anxious? How?
5	When do you feel at your most confident?
6	When do you feel at your least confident?
7	Do you sometimes feel self-conscious?
8	Do you feel like a different person at work from how you feel at home or with friends? If so, what changes?

QUESTIONNAIRE (Cont'd)

9	Do you feel comfortable with how you look?
10	Which are you more aware of: your strengths or your weaknesses?
11	Do you feel powerful? If so, when?
12	Are you aware of your inner critic?
13	When do you feel at your best?
14	Have you ever had a personal coach or mentor?
15	Do you prepare yourself mentally, physically and emotionally before communicating?
16	Do you focus on the other person or people when communicating?

The following pages will show you ways to strengthen your inner engine by:

- Understanding yourself
- Understanding what holds you back
- Identifying ways of preparing yourself mentally and emotionally to create great impact

Read this section, complete the exercises and then revisit these questions to review whether you now feel better equipped to create impact.

UNDERSTANDING YOURSELF

A first step in developing your personal impact and presence is identifying what it is that you want to project to others.

- What are your strengths?
- What are your values? This will provide a clue to what really motivates and inspires you
- How do you want others to see you?
- How do you want to be?

Real presence and impact comes from being congruent at all these levels.

Remember you can't sell yourself unless you know what you are selling.

IDENTIFYING YOUR STRENGTHS

Try some of these exercises to identify your real strengths:

- List **all** your strengths and achievements. Looking back over your life so far, what different things have you enjoyed doing and what were you/are you good at?
- Draw up a personal **SWOT** analysis. Think about how to make the most of the strengths and opportunities available to you
- Ask others what they see as your strengths
- How would your friends and colleagues describe you?
- Ask others to fill in the impact questionnaire for you (see page 44)
- Bring your CV up-to-date and identify what you have to offer others. Create an aspirational CV imagining where you would like to be in five years' time

Strengths	**W**eaknesses
• • •	• • •
Opportunities	**T**hreats
• • •	• • •

YOUR VALUES AND INNER MOTIVATION

Identifying your inner values is important, but may not be something you have given much time to. If you are not clear about your values, use these questions as a prompt:

- List five things you value in yourself and five things you value in others
- Think about a time when you were really motivated: what were you doing and what was it that motivated you?
- Think of five people you really respect (they can be friends, colleagues, leaders, etc). What is it you value about them? We often respect those with similar values to our own, so what does this tell you?... Now jot down some key messages:

The values I want to convey to others are:

1. .... **2.** .... **3.** ....

I want others to see me as someone who ....

The chances are that if you are living your values, your passion will shine through.

STRESS RESPONSES AND IMPACT CONSEQUENCES

To understand impact you need to understand your responses to stress. Stress responses are governed by our primitive brain functions and send us automatically into either a *fight or flight* mode. Handling stress badly can hold us back. These responses are easily recognisable and have a dramatic influence on how we come across.

Stress responses	Impact consequences
Raised heartbeat	• Feeling of panic • Talking too quickly
Blood moves away from peripheral areas	• Unable to focus/listen clearly • May be unable to pick up on cues and responses from your audience
The brain is focused on *fight* or *flight*	• Messages from your long-term memory aren't communicated effectively to your short-term memory, leading to slow thinking and, in extreme cases, stage fright

STRESS RESPONSES AND IMPACT CONSEQUENCES (Cont'd)

Stress responses	Impact consequences
Temperature changes	• From sweating/flushes to feeling extremely cold
Dry mouth	• Voice can be less expressive, can be difficult to get the words out
Emotional reaction	• You become aggressive or submissive; less assertive • Voice tone reflects the emotional reaction • Body language changes into either defensive/protective responses (arms crossed, looking down, closed posture) or more aggressive responses, eg finger pointing

If you can learn to manage these fears you can learn to manage your impact. The first step is to know your inner critic and then develop ways to overcome it.

HANDLING YOUR INNER CRITIC

- Are you your own worst critic?
- Do you remember events which went wrong?
- Do you brood over mistakes?
- Do you ever find yourself procrastinating?
- Do you ever worry about decisions?

If so, don't worry! We all experience the *inner critic* at some time or another.

At its worst, this voice can destroy your confidence, affect your performance and prevent you from reaching your potential.

Often what we hear are messages from the past which may not be helpful to the current situation. As a start, draw a picture of your inner critic, give it a voice and a name. Create an identity separate from your own. It is easier to ignore a negative voice which isn't your own.

MANAGING STRESS

We are hardest on ourselves when under pressure. Interviews, for example, can be enormously stressful, and we can be so focused on trying not to feel nervous that we engage in negative habits, inhibiting our performance and therefore our impact as a result. Some of the following may help to reduce your stress levels:

- Exercise – crucial to managing stress and giving a sense of increased confidence. Try walking home from the station, running up and down stairs for 20 minutes, taking up a sport, dancing, jogging or cycling
- A relaxing warm bath before bed – try adding some lavender oil to aid sleep
- Stretching and/or massage – stretching is a great way to release tense muscles
- Silence – at least once a week try to avoid the over-stimulation of TV, radio and noisy polluted environments. Use the time to put your thoughts in order

MANAGING STRESS (Cont'd)

- Breathing exercises – great when combined with silence
- Sleep – try a combination of the above to ensure a good night's rest
- Food and drink – aim to drink around 1.5 litres of mineral water per day and eat some complex carbohydrates – eg brown rice, plenty of fruit and vegetables
- Diet – try to balance your diet to stabilise the body effectively. When times are really hard, eat plenty of zinc- and magnesium-rich foods, or take a supplement. These important minerals can become depleted under stress

BREATHING

How you breathe is key to your inner impact. You can use breath to control your emotional state and influence your behaviour. Breath also conveys a subliminal message to others, affecting their mood, energy and impression of you. When nervous, you may take in short, shallow breaths that increase your sense of anxiety. This also sends out a message to others, who, in turn, become anxious about your nervousness and focus on that, not on your message.

Try the following breathing exercises to manage nerves and stress. Remember to breathe in and out through your nose to control breathing and slow the system response where adrenaline is present.

1. **Four-step breath** – breathe in, silently counting to four. Hold the breath for a count of four and breathe out for a count of four. Do not hold the breath if you have high blood pressure.
2. **Temperature breath** – notice the change in temperature as you breathe in and out of your nostrils – the air is cool as you inhale and warmer when you exhale. Try to focus on this and let all other thoughts come and go freely.

Always remember, if you feel nervous, breathe **less** not **more.**

VISUALISATION

Visualisation is the process of imagining a future event in your head. When you do this, you are mentally preparing yourself for the outcome that you want. In sport, there is an increasing body of evidence to show the power of visualisation. The old adage, *it's all in the mind*, seems to hold true.

Visualisation is not meditation. It doesn't have to take a long time, but it is a skill. Like all skills, it requires practice so that when you need it, it's there.

Effective visualisation needs to be realistic:

- If you're going to be nervous, you need to visualise yourself as nervous, but concentrate on how you will cope with this
- If you're going to be standing up, eg making a presentation, then you need to visualise standing, as this will make the image more real for your body and mind
- If you're going to be outdoors, you need to practise the visualisation outdoors, etc

Visualisation is a mental rehearsal. When the situation becomes real, you will feel like you've experienced it already. This gives you a sense of confidence and control.

FOCUS ATTENTION

You can't operate at a peak level all the time. So you need to know when you are likely to be at your best and schedule accordingly. That way, you can give the situation your best attention and energy and make the most impact.

Your body operates in complex rhythms. The 24-hour rhythm of the body is called the Circadian rhythm. A typical person who goes to bed at 11.00pm and gets up at 7.00am can expect a post-lunch slump at around 2.00pm and an early evening slump at around 7.00pm. These are not the best times for scheduling important meetings, as your attention will be low. Aim for midday, which is probably the peak operating time for this time clock.

Within the Circadian rhythm is the Ultradian rhythm, a 90-minute cycle during which you reach a peak and then begin to tail off in terms of energy and attention. To keep the focus of others, and ourselves, we should work in 90-minute cycles with a short break.

Find out when you feel at your best and, where possible, schedule your day accordingly.

BREATHING FOR FOCUS

This 10-breath exercise is an important part of impression management. You are able to make clear decisions about how you want others to perceive you. Used by Tibetan monks for 2,000 years, this is a centring exercise. It works by combining imagery/verbal instruction with breathing. You breathe in the qualities you want to present and as you breathe them out… your emotional state will follow. Breathe in and out through the nose – small, natural breaths. No extra effort is required.

- Think of three words that represent how you want to be perceived by others. These words must be **unique** to you and have **meaning** for you; it does not matter what they are, as long as they are **right** for you and **appropriate** for the situation
- Breaths 1-3 — Easy breathing, in and out through the nose, repeating in your mind the first of your three words. The order in which you choose the words may or may not have significance for you
- Breaths 4-6 — As above, but focus on the second of your three words
- Breaths 7-9 — As above, but focus on the third word
- Breath 10 — All three words in the order used for breaths 1-9

You may find that pictures or mental images work just as well, but they **must** be in combination with the breathing.

GETTING IN THE ZONE

This expression is well known from sport and uses preparation skills to help you maximise your performance.

For an athlete, or a performer in the theatre, getting to this place can be achieved through the use of breathing exercises. Controlling the breath means that you are controlling your emotional state and that raises your sense of power and confidence.

Deep breathing is the key to this. But watch out! For most of us, a deep breath can be confused with a big breath and this is going to send adrenaline levels soaring, increasing nerves and anxiety.

Notice how you breathe before you go to sleep, or now as you are reading this book – relaxed and calm. In this state, we hardly breathe at all and this is the state we need to replicate for *getting in the zone*.

GETTING IN THE ZONE

Using exercises like this one can help you achieve your optimum state very quickly – providing you practise the skill regularly so that it feels like second nature when you need it.

Try to incorporate the following exercise into your daily routine, or do it as often as you can to become really familiar with it:

- Sit comfortably, but upright so that your lungs have space to move freely
- Close your eyes
- Breathe in and out through the nose
- Imagine a tiny white feather on the end of your nose
- Breathe steadily, aiming to keep the white feather in place – you hardly need to breathe at all to do this
- Do this for ten minutes and then open your eyes

This is a Zen meditation exercise sometimes used by athletes for achieving 'zone' state. You should feel relaxed and clear-headed. You may feel a little sleepy. This is because we are used to over-breathing as a habit. The more you practise this routine, the better your ability to use it effectively will become.

MOOD WORDS

Athletes use a variety of mental skills to control and optimise performance. **Mood words** are used for focus and management of mental state. In business, you can use this technique to override a reactive response to challenging or stressful situations.

In a 100m race, a sprint athlete may break the race down as follows:

0-10m	10-20m	20-30m	30-40m	40-50m	50-60m
Push	Drive	Forward	Turbo	Pain	Leap

He or she breaks the effort down into manageable segments and controls their emotional state to affect performance. A benefit of this approach is that you have to think about the impact you choose to create, the outcome you want and your strategic approach.

Example: Sally has to deliver a short presentation, written by someone else, to a potential client. She has had little chance to prepare and is nervous. Sally chooses to focus on the emotional response of the audience, rather than the data. She goes through the presentation, slide by slide, and applies different mood words to each slide.

Slide 1	Slide 2	Slide 3	Slide 4	Slide 5
Energy	Reassure	Concern	Optimism	Motivate

CHOOSING YOUR EMOTIONAL STATE

All actors have to learn lines; it's an integral part of the job. This element of it seems to put many people off. Actors are often asked: *'How do you remember all the lines?'*

In fact, actors don't necessarily focus on the lines. They focus on the emotions, knowing how they are going to feel, or how they should be feeling at any time in a play. This gives a clear indication of what it is they should be saying. Then, they are in control.

At work, we are constantly assessing what type of behaviour or approach in a situation would bring about the optimum outcome. Choosing our mood, or emotional state, is a powerful way to achieve this.

For impact and presence, ask yourself the following questions:

- How do I want my audience to feel?
- How do I want to be perceived?

Remember, as an actor does, break down these questions and apply appropriate responses: to specific slides in a presentation, subject areas in a meeting, interview answers or one-to-one communication.

HANDLING REJECTION

We have all experienced rejection, either personally or professionally. It can make us feel devalued and affect the confidence we have in our skills. Positive energy is dynamite for impact and presence. To create it, you need to maintain your self-belief, confidence and motivation.

Here are four tips for handling rejection:

1. Get used to handling rejection. Put yourself in situations where you expect to, or know you will, experience it. This way, you can get used to feeling that it is unimportant. In her book *'Irresistibility'*, Philippa Davies says, *'The more you learn to survive the 'no' the greater your courage and the more you will achieve'*.
2. Don't be bound by fear of failure. Fear of failure can make us deliberately sabotage our chances of success *('No wonder I failed that exam – I did no revision.')*. Try to approach failure as a learning opportunity and next time you'll know exactly how to avoid it.
3. Go for it! Just imagine. If you don't get rejected (this time) you will experience that wonderful life-enhancing event of embracing a challenge and succeeding.
4. Make a decision to benefit from each experience of rejection. Remember the old saying? Don't get mad... get even.

HUMOUR

Being intensely self-focused and self-aware as a means of achieving maximum personal impact is an exciting and valuable journey towards achieving success on your own terms. However, as with all things, perspective is important. Maintaining a sense of humour is critical to accomplishing your goals in this respect.

- Humour is a valuable tool in the fight against negativity; it helps us minimise the pain of rejection or criticism and therefore recover more quickly
- Humour is a great tension-reliever. Many feelings of stress or anxiety can be dispelled by laughter
- Laughing at yourself shows others that you do not take yourself too seriously, which makes you accessible and fun to be around

Be sensitive with humour, laughter and jokes around others. While you can use humour to make yourself more memorable and give an impression of confidence and ease, the timing matters.

REVIEWING IMPACT

Have you ever noticed how we love to replay negative incidents in our minds? The reaction to this scenario might be one you recognise…

John loses his temper with his boss during a meeting. Although the situation is resolved by the end of the meeting, John cannot stop replaying the incident in his mind and wondering if it might affect his career progress. In the middle of the night, he wakes. The incident springs to mind immediately and he cannot sleep for thinking about it. A week later, he sees two people arguing in the street. He relives the argument in the meeting. Five years later, John can still recall this meeting in great detail. The feelings he experienced at that time are immediately clear and he feels the same discomfort he felt then. It's as if it happened yesterday.

For some reason, we love to spend time reviewing the things we have done wrong, or the times we have felt embarrassed. This means that our frame of reference is often negative and becomes a self-fulfilling prophecy.

Making an impact is all about feeling good about yourself, feeling that you have the right to be present. It's important that you put good memories in an accessible place for times when you need that boost of confidence.

CRITICAL INCIDENT EXERCISE

Take a piece of paper and write at the top of it an incident that you can recall in which you felt at your most effective. It might have been in or out of the workplace and it might have happened some years ago. The important thing is that it was a very positive event for you. Try to remember as much detailed information about this incident as you can.

Now do the same with a negative incident (often much easier to recall). Again, as much detail as you can, but be sure to include the following questions:

- What have you learned from this incident?
- What would you do differently next time?
- Did anyone else directly affect the outcome of this incident?

Learn to do this on a regular basis, making it a habit to review positive incidents, and reviewing negative incidents only once or twice to evaluate objectively what you have learned and what you would do differently next time.

The practice of doing this will increase your sense of self-efficacy (a psychological term to describe situation specific self-confidence). The more confident you feel about a situation, the more comfortable you can be with making an unforgettable impact.

DEVELOPING A POSITIVE INNER DIALOGUE

Unfounded fears and worries often stop us performing at our best.

For example, Anil's new job as a business manager meant that he had to present different parts of the business each month and share progress and ideas with the different business teams.

He hated giving presentations and found that beforehand he would have a sleepless night, arrive at the venue feeling tense and then race through his presentation as quickly as possible, making no eye contact with his audience. He knew he could do better, but somehow he couldn't break out of his pattern of fear. The fear was causing a downward spiral of stress, bringing about a less than perfect performance.

Anil worked on all the negative messages he was giving himself and replaced them with positive ones, thus creating a positive inner dialogue. Consciously replacing the negative with positive helped him to be more relaxed and he was able to review his performance. Both he and the teams he worked with saw an improvement.

CHANGING YOUR INNER DIALOGUE

Anil's negative messages	Were replaced by these positive messages
• I'm hopeless at presentations	• I've got the skills and know what to do
• I don't know enough	• I've prepared well and while I don't know everything, I have a reasonable grasp of the subject
• People won't want to listen to me	• The teams want to hear how things are going and enjoy the opportunity of getting together
• I might not be able to answer all the questions	• If I can't answer the questions I can always clarify the issue after the meeting
• People will be judging me	• This is an opportunity for me to get to know the teams and build up a relationship with them

If you have any negative inner dialogues, replace them with more realistic positive messages and turn your performance round. Give your mind positive messages to help you prepare for success.

IDENTIFYING YOUR POWER BASES

- You are more powerful than you think you are. Others are less powerful than you think they are
- Personal power and impact go hand in hand. If you don't feel powerful you will never make an impact
- Power comes in different forms

Type of power	Definition
Position	Based on the position or title someone holds.
Reward	The ability to bestow rewards. (A reward can be something as simple as a piece of praise.)
Coercion	The ability to make someone do something through the threat of negative consequences.
Expert	The knowledge and expertise someone brings to the situation.
Information	Access to information and the perceived value this brings.
Personality	Based on the individual's personality. Are they liked, respected or admired in any way?
Network	Contacts and connections both inside and outside the organisation.

ASSESSING YOUR POWER BASE

Given that many of us do not have formal position power, and are often influencing without formal authority, it is worth assessing your power bases as a way of understanding and developing your impact.

For example, Karen was 24, had been working with her organisation as an accountant for two years, and was asked to present to the senior management team to convince them to invest in a new IT system. Karen had no position power. Her age and lack of experience made her feel nervous about the event. However, when she sat down and reflected on the situation, she recognised that she was very knowledgeable about the system and its benefits. She also had a good network of contacts in the organisation who could help her to prepare for the presentation, and she had been asked because her manager had recommended her. While her position power was low, her knowledge, personality and network power certainly made up for any lack of confidence.

As part of your impact preparation, assess your power bases. They will change from situation to situation but generally you will find that you have more to offer than you initially realised.

FINDING A MENTOR

A mentor is someone who takes a personal interest in an individual, helping them to succeed. Mentors are particularly helpful in the area of impact, as they can often provide help and feedback around issues such as exposure, visibility, networking and organisational politics. All these areas are important if you want to create the right impact and impression in the organisation.

A mentor is usually someone more senior than you in the organisation, and may be from a different business area, so that they can offer impartial advice. A mentor can help develop your impact in several ways:

- Helping to sift through complex organisational issues
- Listening
- Giving constructive feedback on your style
- Guiding communications – who to see, how to present the message
- Giving practical tuition when required
- Providing some clear tips on what to do to develop yourself for the future

CHOOSING A MENTOR

The ideal mentor should be someone you can learn from. You will probably have different mentors at different stages in your career but as a general suggestion, your mentor should be someone:

- You can trust and respect
- Who likes to see people progress
- Who has a wide range of current skills
- Who understands the organisation and its needs
- Who has a good network
- Who can be challenging

If you can think of someone who would be a good mentor, just ask them. Usually mentors are pleased to be asked and get as much out of the relationship as you.

MAINTAINING THE INNER ENGINE

Research shows us that our emotional state influences our behaviour. Our behaviour includes the messages we send to others when we make our impact.

Controlling your emotional state means that you can be in charge of your external behaviour and this sense of control gives a feeling of confidence and freedom.

Part of your ability to manage your emotions comes from a sense of well-being. If you take care of yourself physically, you feel stronger and more able to face new challenges. Also, you have more energy for fun times, and that gives you an increased sense of enjoyment in your life and minimises your stress.

'The man who has confidence in himself gains the confidence of others.'
Hasidic saying

IMPACT FROM THE OUTSIDE IN

IMPACT QUESTIONNAIRE

This questionnaire is intended to provoke self-awareness and reflection on your personal style.

Read through the questions and consider your behaviour.

1	What is the typical expression on your face? How would you describe it?
2	Do you make eye contact with others? Is it direct or indirect? Do your eyebrows move? Do you squint?
3	Would you describe yourself as an energetic or reflective person?
4	Generally, are you 'easy to read' or 'poker-faced'?
5	How would you describe your gestures when communicating? Fluid, smooth, effortless or jerky, laboured? Or non-existent?
6	Are you aware of fiddling or fidgeting when you present?
7	How would you describe your image?
8	Do you pay attention to how you present yourself to others?

IMPACT QUESTIONNAIRE (Cont'd)

9	Do you sometimes look ill at ease?
10	Do you adapt the way you speak to others?
11	Do you find it easy to get along with people?
12	How much attention do you pay to how you look?
13	How much attention do you pay to how other people look?
14	Do you find it easy to listen to people?
15	Do you initiate conversations with others?
16	How aware are you of others' body language and behaviour?

When you have completed this section and tried out some of the exercises, review these questions to see whether your awareness of self and others has improved. If it has, you should be able to experience more control over your physical presence and be in a position to manage your impact from 'the outside in'.

OUTER IMPACT

We have looked at the 'inner engine' of who you are and what you would like to project to others. This section now looks at how to project that image.

Impact from the outside in covers a range of tips, techniques and exercises to develop your physical and vocal presence.

- Eye contact
- Facial expression
- Energy
- Listening
- What we say
- How we say it
- Dress
- Body language
- Posture
- Gestures

IMPACT FROM THE OUTSIDE IN

POSTURE

The key to making a positive impact from a physical perspective is ***ease***. Think about someone who impresses you with their style and confidence. Chances are they have an upright, confident posture.

Before communicating with anyone, try to take a few seconds to check how you feel. Ask yourself: 'Do I feel tense anywhere? Does it show?'

If the answer is yes, then shake out the tension. Try the following:

- Shake your hands vigorously for a few minutes
- Scrunch your body, face, everything as tight as you can – hold for a count of five and then let everything go
- Take a five minute brisk walk
- Stretch, yawn

Ease in the body suggests confidence. It also sends a positive message to the body that all is well. Posture is all about habits. Change your habits by reminding yourself constantly that with better posture you look stronger. You make a more dynamic impact and create far more energy for yourself when you get rid of tension and stand up. Remember, *gravitas* is anti-gravity.

Good posture can also help to manage back pain, headaches, muscular tension and make you appear about 10lbs lighter.

TECHNIQUES FOR IMPROVING PHYSICAL PRESENCE

There are a number of practitioners working with the body to create the impression of ease and confidence. If you experience a lot of tension, or are aware that your posture needs work, consider using one of these methods to improve your immediate impact. Details of practitioners can be found at the back of the book.

Feldenkrais	A slow and gentle method of working with the body to overcome physical limitations brought on by stress, bad habits, accidents (eg sport injuries) or illness. It helps people perform and feel better both physically and mentally.
Alexander Technique	This technique is used by actors, musicians and sports people to maximise energy and minimise tension in the body. It's a shortcut to achieving personal presence owing to the confident, easy impression it allows you to create.
Pilates	Initially used by dancers as a means of improving flexibility and strength, Pilates is now very much part of any gym exercise programme, owing to its emphasis on strength and postural poise, without building muscular bulk.

These disciplines have a specific postural focus, but you might also try yoga, T'ai Chi, dance classes or regular workouts in the gym (making sure that you always check your posture in the mirror, of course!) to improve the energy in your body and the impression of confidence in the way you sit, stand and walk.

IMPACT FROM THE OUTSIDE IN

GESTURE

If you are worrying about your hands, you are not able to listen effectively or give anyone your full attention.

Research in social psychology suggests that larger, expansive gestures imply a confident person, while small, close to the body gestures imply the opposite.

- Practise gesturing in front of a mirror. This may feel awkward at first but, once you feel less self-conscious, it will prove valuable to your awareness of your impact on others
- Practise standing with your arms hanging by your side. This drains tension away from your shoulders and, once mastered, gives an easy, confident impression
- Keep gestures fluid and easy – jerky or rapid movements suggest lack of confidence
- Try talking with your hands kept at about waist height –TV journalists use this to show expressivity in their movements, while looking confident and engaged
- Do not keep change or keys in pockets
- Don't put both hands in pockets (one may be acceptable)
- Don't fidget – avoid fiddling with hair, pens, clothing, earrings, etc
- If you have a favourite gesture, don't use it more than three times in succession as it will become a distraction

HANDSHAKE

When you shake hands with someone, you send out a strong message about your confidence and you receive a message about theirs.

- Make sure that your handshake is strong and firm
- Give men and women the same handshake, unless there are cultural implications
- Sweaty palms can be very off-putting – use a little unscented anti-perspirant deodorant on your palms to prevent sweating
- Never wipe your hands on your trousers in view of others before shaking hands
- Maintain eye contact – make sure that you instruct yourself to make positive eye contact to support the confidence in your grip
- If the other person offers a limp, weak handshake, consider matching the style of that rather than expecting to 'shake them out of it' with your own firm grip
- Notice handshake styles of public figures and see if you can identify one that might be appropriate for you to try
- Be aware that every context is different and may require that the style of your handshake vary from person to person in different situations

EYE CONTACT

In Western society eye contact has great importance. We often use it to make judgements about people's honesty and commitment, and may not always trust people who don't *look us in the eye*.

You don't need to directly 'eyeball' someone, as this can be off-putting, so looking at a spot between their eyebrows can help.

Remember, though, that in some cultures eye contact can be disrespectful.

Your eyes provide wonderful signals to others about your emotional and mental state and it is important to be aware of their impact.

There are times when good eye contact is particularly impactful:

- In presentations – always scan the audience so that you have made eye contact with as many people as possible
- Shaking hands – when shaking hands always look at the other person with a good steady gaze
- When making a point – when you want to make a point or recommendation always make eye contact with the other person; it shows your belief and commitment

IMPACT FROM THE OUTSIDE IN

CREATING ATMOSPHERE

Human beings are generally sensitive to atmosphere. We all have experience of walking into a room where the atmosphere is tense or angry; equally we find comfort and pleasure in visiting places where the atmosphere is calm and soothing, or warm and friendly. This energy field is everywhere and we tend to be affected by it.

When you are planning your impact, you can make decisions about what kind of atmosphere you want to create. In the workplace, environment has been shown to impact on performance by as much as 30%.

Creating atmosphere is a choice. Think of a time when you have chosen to be assertive, eg when complaining in a restaurant. This creates an atmosphere or energy field around you. You can have the same result anywhere. You simply need to choose your energy.

Consider the following:

- Is the situation formal or informal?
- How do you want people to feel?
- How are you feeling and what will you be changing to create the right atmosphere?

IMPACT FROM THE OUTSIDE IN

ENJOYING YOUR SPACE

Creating impact and presence can be easier when you are in familiar, comfortable surroundings. You appear confident 'in your space'.

However, in an unfamiliar environment, eg a meeting with a prospective client at their premises, a presentation, business pitch or an interview, you may feel and appear uncomfortable, uneasy or nervous.

Try the following tips to maximise your impact and feeling of confidence in new and unfamiliar environments:

- Ensure your focus is directed around you. Take in as much detail about your surroundings as you can, including the colour of the walls, flooring, etc
- Talk to yourself to divert from any nervousness and to reinforce confidence in the new environment, eg *'I like this room. It is bright and warm. The view from the window looks lovely. It feels really welcoming in here – I feel quite at home'*
- Be aware of the depth and breadth of your peripheral vision
- Create space around you by visualising yourself in a bubble or circle that allows you to include others, or say to yourself, *'This is my space'*

RAPPORT

Rapport is often referred to as 'being on the same wavelength'. When people have rapport, they understand each other and get on well. It is a vital factor in customer service and successful business relationships.

When people have good rapport they often 'mirror' behaviour on a number of different levels:

- Through their body language and non-verbal communication
- Through their energy and pace, which is often reflected in the speed and tone of their voice
- Through the content and language of what they are saying

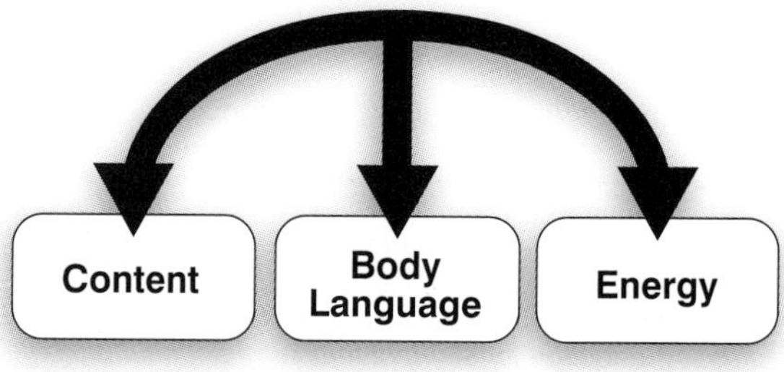

MATCHING AND MIRRORING

Next time you want to make an impact, try to relax and match the other person. This doesn't mean mimicking them exactly, but it does mean paying attention to what they are doing:

- If they are sitting make sure you sit down so that you are at the same level
- Match your voice and energy
- Use similar body language

Once you achieve rapport this will happen naturally, so you are only trying to enhance what is a natural phenomenon.

If you are always aware of these cues, you will be able to identify when people have good rapport or not, just by watching their body language for signs of matching or mirroring.

MATCHING ENERGY LEVELS

Creating rapport through body language is important, but equally valuable is the ability to match others in terms of their energy and pace.

Some people are fast-paced. They talk quickly, use lots of gestures, have a wide range of facial expressions and are generally energetic in nature.

Other people are slower paced. They are more reflective, talk at a more measured pace, like time to think things through and are not as expressive through gestures and facial expressions.

Which are you?

Be aware that energy levels can change under stress. Often in presentations, people speed up and even gabble, losing the richness and texture of their voice. If this happens to you, do something to break up the pattern: take a drink from a glass of water, breathe slowly and deeply, take a pause and move on at a more acceptable energy level.

If you want to create more impact with others, try to match their energy level. This may mean slowing down a little, or adding a bit more energy to your personal presentation style.

IMPACT FROM THE OUTSIDE IN

CREATING RAPPORT THROUGH CONTENT AND LANGUAGE

People have different ways of thinking and processing their ideas. If you can be aware of your style and that of others, you can learn to flex your style to increase rapport, impact and understanding.

The area of NLP (Neuro Linguistic Programming) provides some insight into different thinking styles.

There are three main styles, visual, auditory and kinaesthetic. You can pick up cues about people's style from what they say:

Visual	Auditory	Kinaesthetic
I can see my way clearly. I like to keep an eye on things. Do you get the picture?	I like to tune in to new ideas. I hear what you say. I'll keep my ear to the ground.	I like to get the feel of things. I'm feeling the pressure of life. We need to get to grips with the issue.

FLEXING YOUR STYLE

Imagine selling a car to someone:

- A visual person will be impressed by the look of the car
- An auditory person by the sound of the engine
- A kinaesthetic person by the feel of the upholstery

If you can listen to, and match, someone else's preferred thinking style, it will enhance your communication and influencing skills. In a presentation you can create greater impact by using a range of styles to reflect the likely make-up of the audience.

You can also match the language of the other person in different ways:

- Use their jargon not yours
- Reflect back their words, eg *'You were impressed by the last model?' 'You seem very satisfied with the service provided.' 'You said you wanted a model which offers a smooth ride'*
- Use the same words and phrases. For example, don't use words like 'empowerment' if you know people will groan or switch off

IMPACT FROM THE OUTSIDE IN

LISTENING

Research shows that successful sales people spend more time listening and asking questions than they do making statements, so listening has a lot to offer.

You can listen to the **facts** that people are saying at different levels, to the **feelings** they are expressing and to the **intentions** which may be hidden amongst the words.

Facts	The context of the story, logical progression, words used and arguments put forward.
Feelings	Feelings may be labelled and talked about but often you can pick these up from voice tone, pace and body language. Small signals such as sighs, shrugs, changes in posture and facial expression can tell you a lot, so listen with your eyes as well as your ears.
Intentions	You can often pick up information about someone's intentions while they are talking. They may become more animated at certain parts of the story, they may present ideas, options and problems and also possible solutions.

It is important to listen at all these levels in order to fully understand the other person. Summarising and reflecting back what you have heard then demonstrates that you are interested, and also provides you with the opportunity either to ask more questions or move the conversation on to a new topic.

QUESTIONING

Good questioning skills are equally essential.

Good questioners:

- Show their interest
- Ask questions which provide them with useful information
- Make the other person feel valued
- Demonstrate understanding

Some of the most useful questions are listed on the next page

QUESTIONING

Type of question	When to use it	Example
Open	• To establish rapport • To gain background information • To explore ideas/opinions and attitudes	*Tell me about your role.* *What approach do you take?* *What is your opinion on…?*
Probing	• To show interest • To dig a bit deeper and explore an issue in more detail • To show understanding	*What makes you say that?* *I'm really interested in X, tell me more.*
Reflective	• To check understanding • To explore a topic in more depth • To reflect back facts and feelings	*You seem very happy with things, am I right?* *So, your challenge is managing the team?*
Clarifying	• To test understanding	*So what you are saying is…* *Can you just clarify your situation?*

The ability to ask questions well can help you to acquire an air of authority and establish greater rapport.

IMPACT FROM THE OUTSIDE IN

'YES, AND ...'

'Yes... but' is like saying *'No'*. For true positive impact, use *'Yes...and'*. This encourages others to offer input and ideas and makes you appear dynamic, open-minded and open-hearted, excellent qualities to demonstrate when trying to make a positive impact on influencing others.

Scenario 1

Sunita approaches her manager with a suggestion for improving employee efficiency in the office by reorganising the desk layout. Sunita's manager is not keen. His response is: *'No, Sunita. It's a waste of time. I don't think it'll work and it'll cause too many complaints.'*

Scenario 2

Sunita's manager has received feedback suggesting that he needs to take a more positive, proactive approach in management. So he tries the following: *'**Yes**, we could make some changes, **but** have you thought about the disruption this will cause and the complaints the team will make?'*

Scenario 3

Sunita has a new manager. She has similar reservations, but her response is this: *'**Yes**, great idea Sunita, **and** we could make the changes at the weekend with volunteers. We can try it for, say, six weeks and if it doesn't work out, we can change back.'*

SIMPLICITY AND CLARITY

- To make a powerful impact when communicating, identify the essence of your message. Try, in your mind, to encapsulate your message as a headline and return to it whenever you find yourself going off track
- Try to minimise the use of hedges and qualifiers when you speak. The quality of a simple and clear message is easily destroyed by adding 'quite, really, very' or 'umms and uhhs'

Here's an example:

Mike is nervous as he delivers his team review of the last financial quarter.

'Umm, good morning everyone and umm, what I'd really like to say is thanks for finding the time to come along this morning. It's umm, well, it's been quite an eventful quarter and uhh, we are now feeling really very optimistic about umm, the next, umm, few months.'

This approach has more impact:

'Good morning ladies and gentlemen and welcome. Thank you for coming this morning to review our previous quarter and learn how we plan to move forward. It has been eventful, and this extraordinary period has allowed us to move forward into the next quarter with great optimism.'

BEING HEARD

When you have a message to deliver, whether to an audience of one person or a thousand people, it must be heard.

A baby uses about 28 notes, or four octaves, in its vocal range, allowing it to sound expressive and skilfully deliver a message with no words. As adults, we may use as few as two or three notes in the vocal range. Imagine attending a concert where the orchestra only played two or three notes. A good way to fall asleep and ensure a forgettable performance!

To avoid this in your communication, try thinking about ways in which you can vary the range of your voice to ensure that your 'concert performance' is dynamic and memorable.

The **LASER** model will help you remember what you need to focus on when delivering a message:

Loudness
Articulation
Speed
Emphasis
Range

Use the acronym to ensure that your messages are **LASER** sharp and clear and get straight to the heart of your audience.

TIPS FOR OPTIMISING YOUR VOICE

- Always drink plenty of water. The voice dries easily when you talk a lot, in a meeting, making a presentation or in a networking event
- Try not to clear your throat before you start to speak. This can lead to an irritating and distracting habit, but also the more you clear the throat of excess mucus, the more mucus the throat creates as a means of coating the vocal folds. If you must, have one good cough and then drink water. This will make the mucus more fluid and distract you less
- Try not to smoke. Smoking burns the vocal folds and can change voice quality, impair vocal flexibility, dry out the voice and provoke distracting coughing habits
- Try to minimise intake of dairy products as they can create phlegm

We can often guess a person's approximate age by listening to their voice. This is because the cartilage in the pharynx calcifies (turns to bone) with lack of use. So if you don't want your voice to give away your age, make sure it is well-exercised to maintain flexibility.

SOUNDING AUTHENTIC

For a message to be heard, understood and remembered, it needs to be delivered with sincerity and credibility. Sounding authentic is critical to your message. Sometimes you can passionately believe in what you are saying, but your voice, owing to lack of effort and use, can let you down. You don't 'sound' like you mean it – like you are connected to what you say. So, if your voice is going to be an asset to your impact, it may need a little work.

The voice is like an orchestral wind instrument. It has a *power source* – breath; a *resonator* – the pharynx and other spaces in the body where sound reverberates; and a *reed* – the vocal folds, which vibrate incredibly fast to produce sound.

Playing an instrument well needs practice. Try the following exercises to keep your voice on top form. Think of doing them as part of your daily routine. They can easily be done in the shower or in the car on the way to work or to a meeting. You should notice the benefits quite quickly.

It may sound like a cliché, but it's not so much *what* we say as *how* we say it.

VOICE WORKOUT

1. Yawn freely two or three times to release tension and open the throat.
2. Give yourself a bear hug and inhale deeply through the nose. You should feel your ribs and back stretching.
3. Stand with good posture – tall and open physically. Place one hand on your tummy. Inhale through the nose and exhale making an 'fff' or 'sss' sound until you run out of breath. You should feel your tummy contracting with the effort. These are the muscles you should feel working for you when you are speaking.
4. Do some humming. Gentle humming on any note that feels comfortable will warm the vocal folds and get them ready for action. Gradually change the note up and down the range of your voice but stay within a comfortable range.

IMPACT FROM THE OUTSIDE IN

VOICE WORKOUT (Cont'd)

5. Repeat step three, but this time breathe out, making a 'vvv' or 'zzz' sound. (Any note that feels comfortable will suit this exercise).
6. Play around with the pitch range of your voice, swooping up and down through the notes as far as you can without straining.
7. Pull some amazing faces! Stretch the muscles of the face to minimise tension and ensure expressivity.
8. Blow air through the lips like a horse and then smack the lips together.
9. Resurrect some childhood tongue twisters and play with them every day!

MODELLING IMPACT

LEARNING FROM OTHERS

'To really know someone you must first walk a mile in their moccasins.' **Indian proverb**

It is also useful to model others as a way of acquiring a new skill.

Most of us have role models, who express some behaviour, value or attitude that we aspire to. These role models may change at different stages in our lives but they will have made an impact on us in some way.

Modelling another's behaviour can be useful in learning any new skill, eg:

- Presentation skills
- Generating commitment
- Building trust
- Selling and influencing, etc

MODELLING IN PRACTICE

Think about an impact skill you would like to develop and identify someone who does this well.

- What is it that they do to make this impact? Try to deconstruct the different aspects of their behaviour, speech and body language
- Talk to them about how they make an impact. They may not be aware of what they do that makes them a success, so be specific in your questions and ask them about their skills, mental state and motivations. Suggest that they imagine a time when they were demonstrating this skill and ask them what inspires them, what they are thinking and what is important to them
- Identify what you can learn from others, both from the performance and the values, beliefs and attitudes that drive it. Find ways of building these elements into your repertoire of behaviours and monitor your own performance – you should see an improvement

Developing Your Personal Brand

IDENTIFYING YOUR BRAND

Just as organisations create a brand image, we need to think of ourselves as brands and understand what we stand for and what sort of impact and presence we want to create.

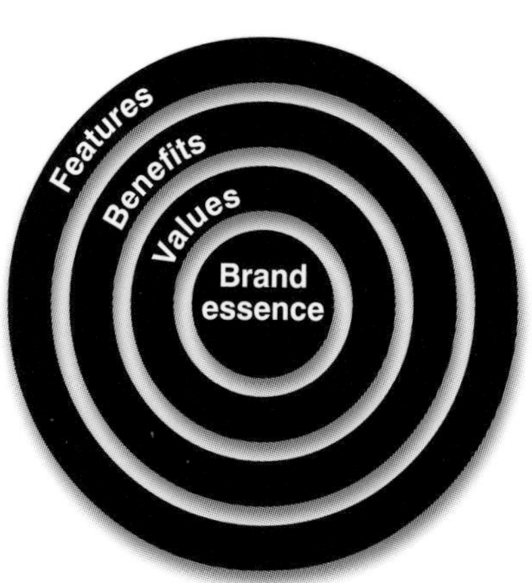

Well known organisations such as Pizza Express and easyJet have strong brands that they work on at all levels, so that there is real congruence between the internal values and the front-line behaviour experienced by the customer.

The challenge therefore is to understand what your personal brand stands for and present yourself in a way that expresses your core values.

CREATING YOUR BRAND IDENTITY

First you need to have an offer that people really want; then you can build a brand around it.

The essence of the brand is its vision and meaning, for example:

Harley Davidson do not sell motor cycles; its brand vision is: *'We fulfil dreams.'*
The vision behind the creation of Pizza Express in 1965 was to...*'Serve the world with style'* and this still drives the company today.

Your brand identity is what people will remember you by; it should be clear in everything you do.

A creative way to define your brand identity is to sit down with a pile of magazines and create a collage to represent how you would like to project yourself to the world. When you have completed it, look at the collage and identify just what it is saying about you and your brand.

CREATING YOUR BRAND STATEMENT

- Think about what you really value about your work and what you offer that is unique to you
- Use your collage to draw out what it is you want your brand to express

From this create a sentence which can define your brand.

A management development colleague described her brand essence as: *'I develop potential'*. This came through in all aspects of her brand, her personal values, the benefits she offered and what she did. It was expressed to her customers through her dedication and her friendly and professional approach.

Features (what you offer – the front-line expression of your brand)	**Benefits** (the benefits of working with you)	**Values** (your personal values)	**Brand essence**
• High quality professional delivery • Relevant tailored materials • Individual, one-to-one time • A personal approach	• Increased confidence • Improvements in work • Increased motivation • Personal development	• People matter • Everyone has potential • Integrity • Personal change is possible	To develop potential

CREATE YOUR OWN BRAND

Fill in the table below and create your own brand.

Features (what you offer – the front-line expression of your brand)	**Benefits** (the benefits of working with you)	**Values** (your personal values)	**Brand essence**

Just as a brand has to live in the minds of the consumers, your brand has to live in the minds of those you meet, so work on turning your brand values into front-line behaviours.

DEVELOPING BRAND AWARENESS

Good brands are supported by tactical advertising and marketing and PR campaigns. How good is your brand awareness? And how do you create it?

Here are a few tips:

- Choose clothes and accessories that reflect you as your brand
- Always have your business card with you
- Follow up on meetings and requests for help
- If you are freelance or self-employed, make sure that all your business materials powerfully mirror your overall branding
- Tell people about what you do well

You are your own best marketing tool.

YOUR BRAND IMAGE

The impact of your image can be considered in three ways:

1. Self-image
2. Projected image
3. Received image

It is important that there is congruence between them. Like any brand, if the customer does not recognise what the brand has to offer, it will fail.

To increase self-image and ensure that your visual impact is how you want it to be, you need to be aware of and honest about your strengths, what suits you, and how to use this for maximum impact.

You also need to consider your audience: will your image be well received or do you need to adapt it in some way?

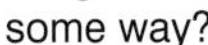

PACKAGING THE BRAND

UNDRESSED

The image you choose to project makes a statement about who you are. The first impression you create is a lasting one and it's important to feel confident in your choices.

Here are some simple rules:

- **Teeth** – regular check-ups at the dentist will ensure that your smile makes a great impact. Check your teeth after meals for unattractive bits of food
- **Skin** – keep the skin moisturised; this applies to men and women. Dry, flaky skin does not enhance a positive first impression
- **Smell** – keep clean and fresh. You don't have to invest in expensive perfumes, but clothes and hair especially need to have a fresh, clean appearance and smell
- **Hair** – a good haircut helps increase confidence and sends a strong message of self-care. This is especially important for men. Straggly ends and an unkempt hairstyle may give off the wrong impression about how you approach business. And ladies? Keep long hair tied back and all hair off the face or away from the eyes

PACKAGING THE BRAND

DRESSED

- **Shoes** – a great outfit and hairstyle can be spoilt by a dirty or down-at-heel pair of shoes. Pay attention to wear and tear on footwear and take action. Try to keep footwear as dark, or darker, than the hemline of your clothes to ensure a long line and keep the attention of your audience on your face, not your feet
- **Clothes** – nothing too tight or too baggy. You will feel uncomfortable with your image choices and suffer a lack of confidence as a result. Be honest about your real shape and enhance it with properly fitting clothes
- Take someone shopping with you who will be honest and sensitive about your choices. We are not always the best judge of our own look, so get another opinion or seek out a personal shopper in a department store who will advise you on styles and colours
- 80% of our visual attention is focused on the 'newscaster' area – ie the head and shoulders. Make sure that you pay particular attention to this area as it establishes your personal style

The following pages have general guidelines for men and women.

MEN

Think about the style that is appropriate for your corporate environment. Do you match the style? How do you feel your image compares with your colleagues? What do you like about your dress style? What would you change; what's stopping you from changing it?

Consider the following when choosing your clothes:

- **Your shape and size** – try to buy a style that flatters rather than panders to current fashions
- **Your colouring** – check your wardrobe for items that you haven't worn much, or wear if there is nothing else available. Do you like the colour or pattern? Some clothes will feel great and this is often because we instinctively know the colour is right. Ask for some advice on colour from a trusted friend or partner. Alternatively, find an image consultant who will advise you on what colours are right for you
- **Your personal style** – do you feel at home in a suit or more comfortable in smart casual clothing? Both can be appropriate in today's working environment

Allow your shirts and ties to show your creative side, but don't let wild patterns or designs distract from you. Remember, your clothes are there to enhance your image. Aim to be remembered for who you are, not what you wear.

WOMEN

Research* shows that 93% of Personnel and Finance Directors interviewed felt that a woman's personal image was important to her career development and success.

Honouring our individual style seems to be crucial to image success, rather than slavishly following the current fashion trends. We may be creative, traditional, formal or casual, but each style can look professional, sophisticated and make an impact.

Basic rules for professional women:

- **Colour** – take professional advice on what colours make you look good, or take a creative and stylish friend shopping with you
- Be honest about your **body shape** and dress accordingly – nothing too tight or too baggy
- Be cautious with **skirt length** – too short may make you feel self-conscious and send the wrong message; just below the knee is almost always unflattering and too long shortens everyone. Invest in a dressmaker to make your hemline right for you
- Wear stylish but comfortable **shoes**. Appearing confident while wincing with the pain of pinched feet is an uphill struggle

* Mary Spillane, *Branding Yourself*, Pan, 2000

FIRST IMPRESSIONS

What impression do others form of you when they first meet you?

Try the following. Use a mirror, preferably full-length, to see what choices you make:

- Smile and introduce yourself. It may seem strange to try out different facial expressions in the mirror, but have a go and see what impression you feel you give
- Notice your favoured or preferred expressions. Do you tend to smile, frown, look tense, dreamy, etc? How do you want to look? Try it out
- How do you choose to stand? Do you look uncomfortable or at ease? Apologetic or confident? What do you look like when you stand tall and confidently proffer your hand and smile? Try it out

Remember, this is not intended to be an exercise in wishing you looked different. This is about realistically appraising your initial impact on others. If you don't do it, be aware that other people are doing it for you all the time. Get ahead of the game and feel that you can adapt your behaviour to suit the situation. It's an instant confidence boost.

EXTENDING YOUR BRAND

Living and expressing your brand is essential in creating impact and presence, but it is also important to adapt to your environment.

McDonald's initially failed in working globally because they tried to replicate their restaurants on a global basis without taking account of cross-cultural differences. On the other hand, Virgin has been able to straddle a number of markets, Virgin Atlantic, Virgin Express, Virgin Direct, Virgin Travelstore, Virgin One … just to name a few.

In the same way, it is important to recognise that you may need to adapt slightly for different people and environments.

Think about your dress, the way you present your ideas, the language you use and the degree of formality you use.

Part of your impact preparation should be to find out as much as you can about your audience and plan to adapt and extend your brand accordingly.

NOTES

ADAPTING TO THE ENVIRONMENT

MEETINGS

Preparing for and making the most of any meeting is important. It is your chance to make an impact and influence others.

- Arrive early and make sure you sit in a central position where you have the eye of the chair and can be seen by the group
- Be organised, create some space for yourself by laying out any relevant papers
- Use body language, remembering to lean forward and signal when you want to speak
- Look interested; people will notice if you are looking bored or day-dreaming
- Try to speak early: it will give you confidence and people will know you are there
- Build on others' ideas and pick up on any links to your own ideas
- Summarising the points made so far helps to show you are listening, including others and getting your ideas across
- Always speak clearly and to the point
- If you are making recommendations, don't make too many as it can dilute your overall argument
- Think about how to dress, especially if you are visiting a client's office. What is their dress code, and how should you adapt your style?

MAKING SMALL TALK WORK FOR YOU

In networking meetings and client events the challenge is to make an impact with people you don't know, but want to impress in some way. Here are a few tips:

- Check the invitation list. Is there anyone you know you would like to meet?
- Don't just say your name; have your 15-second pitch prepared (see page 89)
- Be relaxed and at ease. It will help others to feel the same
- If you are meeting someone again, try to bring something about them and your last meeting into the conversation
- Show you are interested by asking questions and paying attention. A good conversationalist is usually a good listener
- Find some common ground that you can both talk about
- Have a positive handshake
- Have your business card with you and present it face upwards. When you receive a card from someone else, look at the person so that you can connect their name and face
- Wear your badge on the right side of your jacket so that other people's eyes will be drawn to it when they shake your hand
- Always use people's names in conversation

REMEMBERING NAMES

Sarah was at a networking party. She was chatting to a colleague when a client from a company that she had worked for previously approached her and said, *'Hi, Sarah. How are you?'* It was an awful moment. Although she could remember plenty of details about their working relationship, she could not remember the client's name. Feeling embarrassed, she tried to cover up by talking about the many different projects they had worked on together. Just then, Sarah's boss arrived expecting to be introduced...

Here are some tips for managing names in situations like this.

- Own up! Say straight away, *'I am so sorry. I remember so many details about you and our time together, but I am hopeless with names. Please remind me of yours.'*
- NEVER say to a person, vaguely, *'Oh... what's your name?'* or, *'And your name is/was...?'* This will make them feel worthless – and create a negative impact
- When you receive a business card, write some details or a description of the person on the back of the card for reference. File all cards and refer to them when you know you are attending an event where that person is likely to appear
- For better recall, use a mnemonic (memory device) like rhyming their name with something close to it, or associating their name with an image or famous character

CREATING YOUR 15-SECOND WINNING INTRODUCTION

'When you meet someone for the first time, you have the opportunity to make your mark. Everything about you is intensified and exaggerated – your manner, your gestures, voice and facial expression. Don't just passively submit to examination; leave a lasting impression.'
Mary Mitchell, *The First Five Minutes*, John Wiley, 1998

Prepare and practise a winning introduction stating:

- **Who you are**
- **What you do**
- **What you have to offer**

If you know what you want to say you will have more chance of introducing yourself in a confident and memorable manner.

PRESENTATIONS

MANAGING CONTENT

To add extra impact and spice to your presentations consider the following points.

Have a clear objective:

- Explain the objective of the presentation
- Think about it in terms of the audience – what's in it for them?
- What do you want the presentation to achieve?

Is your opening going to make an impact?

- Memorise and practise it
- Let the audience know who you are
- Remember that first impressions shape the tone of the whole presentation

Is your closing impactful?

- Have a clear summary which you can memorise
- Use the close to summarise your key messages
- What do you want the audience to do next? Let them know if you want a response from them or any specific action

Finally, go through your material with a trusted colleague for honest feedback.

PRESENTATIONS

MANAGING PEOPLE

Manage your audience:

- Prepare by thinking about the audience and adapting the presentation to their needs
- Let your content serve your audience's needs not your own
- Get them involved by planning the questions you want to ask them
- If appropriate, get them to work in groups or pairs so that they feel more comfortable sharing their ideas
- Use their language and avoid jargon which may alienate them

Manage yourself:

- Make sure you are prepared
- Don't just plan the content of the presentation; spend time thinking about how you will put it across
- Work on your pace, voice tone and body language so that you will be able to make maximum impact
- Wear something you feel good in
- Practise visualisation (see page 25) to help you prepare for a positive experience
- Take the floor with confidence. Stand firm, look at the audience, use open gestures and smile

ADAPTING TO THE ENVIRONMENT

PRESENTATIONS

ADDING ZEST

Maintaining the interest of an audience is not easy given the fact that our attention span is pretty low, and that people forget 75% of what they hear within 24 hours. Add impact boosters to sustain energy and keep the messages and ideas fresh in their minds.

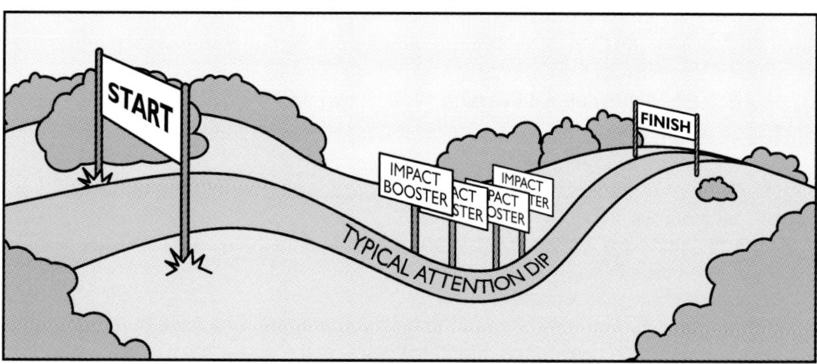

PRESENTATIONS

TIPS FOR ADDING ZEST

So how do you keep the audience alert? Here are a few ideas for impact boosters:

- Use clear visual aids, add in quotes and visuals where appropriate
- Think of clever ways to present figures; pie charts and bar charts work much better than a sea of numbers
- Tell stories and give examples to bring the presentation alive
- Avoid death by PowerPoint by using the flip chart and bringing along other visual aids
- Rather than talking at the audience, ask questions and get them involved
- In a long presentation, add in some exercises to make the audience active
- Refer to people by name or by their department
- Tailor what you say so that you can show you understand the audience
- Use humour if appropriate

'The exact words that you use are far less important than the energy, intensity and conviction with which you use them.' **Jules Rose**

DEALING WITH AN AUDIENCE

Dealing with an audience, whether one person or a thousand, can be scary. No audience is ever the same; it is not possible to predict how they will respond, what questions they will ask (if any), whether they will seem warm and responsive or cold and uninterested. In any event, how they seem to respond is not necessarily consistent with how they really feel. It's pretty confusing. Actors are used to facing this challenge on a daily basis and have some useful techniques for handling it.

- Try not to 'make up' what an audience is feeling. While we can try to get a sense of audience response by observing body language and behaviour, it is impossible to know for sure what's going on in their minds. Instead, try this:
- Endow your audience with one of the following behaviours. Make this decision as you look at them and remind yourself of it if you feel any uncertainty at any time during your communication. Try one of the following, or come up with some of your own. Endow them with:

1. Anticipation and excitement **2.** Warmth **3.** Intelligence **4.** Integrity **5.** Humour

Or, simply make the decision that you like them. This will then show in your behaviour.

THE KIPPER TIE TECHNIQUE FOR POWERFUL PRESENTATIONS

If you are asked to make an off the cuff presentation and don't have much time to prepare, try this technique.

It's called the *kipper tie* technique because it is a mixture of convergent and divergent thinking; it's amazing what you can do when you apply a bit of creative thinking to the situation.

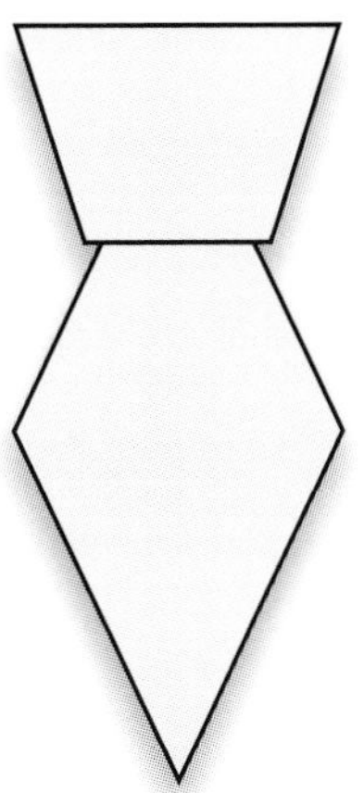

1. Brainstorm all the angles you take on the topic
2. Hone your ideas down to one specific topic
3. Now brainstorm everything you know about this topic
4. Now hone this down to no more than five key points with a clear beginning, middle and end

IMPACT AND INFLUENCING

People often fail when they try to influence because they put all their effort into preparing the argument and looking at how to win their corner, rather than thinking about the wider picture of influencing. To influence with impact requires preparation time:

- Look at how you can create a win-win situation
- Put yourself in the shoes of the other person. What are their needs and concerns? Try to connect with them on an emotional level
- Identify the WIIFT (What's In It For Them)
- Identify areas of common ground so that you can start the discussion off by looking at areas of similarity
- Think about how to create rapport with the other person through your dress, language and posture
- Establish your credibility, through your work, your contacts and networks
- Provide compelling evidence for your case. Use stories, metaphors and analogies to make your ideas come alive

INTERVIEW IMPACT

Interview preparation:

- Find out as much as you can about the atmosphere of the company. Check out their materials and their website. If you get the chance, hang out in the reception area and observe employees coming and going. This is a great way to detail corporate image and mood
- Get a colleague to give you a really tough 'dry run', asking challenging questions that you have prepared, and some that you haven't!
- Plan how to manage your nerves. (This is a good time to put into practice some of the techniques from other sections of the book)

Initial impact:

- Plan your outfit to fit with the corporate environment and be sure that you are feeling and looking at your best
- Smile! Make the interviewer feel you are glad to be there
- Ensure your handshake is confident and firm with great eye contact

ADAPTING TO THE ENVIRONMENT

IN THE INTERVIEW

- Aim to show your enthusiasm, rather than attempt to appear laid back or 'cool'
- Sit up – use 'up' energy and focus on open body language
- Match the interviewer's energy, both physical and vocal
- Maintain eye contact
- Listen without interruption when the interviewer is speaking
- Blow your own trumpet – loud and proud. The interviewer will not assume that you are being modest. However, don't exaggerate or claim experience you don't have!
- Use pause to buy thinking time as you prepare your answers during the interview. This will help you mentally, but also give the impression that your answers are thoughtful and considered, rather than rehearsed
- Have some questions prepared – but not about salary or the package on offer. It's important not to give the impression that the job is attractive because of the money
- Enhance your chances of being memorable by writing the interviewer a note after the interview thanking them for the experience and for their time. This makes a real impact as almost no one bothers to do it
- Don't forget to analyse what you did well and what you might do differently in future interviews

IMPACT AND PROMOTION

DON'T FALL OFF THE RAILS

Research from The Centre of Creative Leadership has identified that managers who are successful in the early stages of their careers can literally derail as they move into more senior positions. This is because making impact as a young manager requires a different set of skills, as the table below illustrates.

Success in early management positions is often associated with:	Success in more senior leadership positions is often associated with:
• Independence	• Being a team player
• Ability to control short-term results	• Having longer-term strategic vision
• Creativity	• Managing the creativity of others
• Ambition and high standards	• Self-esteem
• Speciality strength	• General management skills
• Being contentious – taking a stand	• Creating unity and cohesion

IMPACT AND PROMOTION

DON'T FALL OFF THE RAILS

The research found that, for the most part, managers who derailed did so because:

- They had difficulty in building and leading teams
- They were unable to change and adapt during transitions
- They failed to meet business objectives
- They didn't follow through on ideas
- They treated others unfairly
- They were over-dependent on others for their success

If you want to develop your career and your impact it may be worth assessing your skills, abilities and attitudes towards leadership so that you are able to make the transition to more senior positions.

IMPACT THE ASSERTIVE WAY

Assertiveness and impact go hand-in-hand because, put simply, you will fail to make a positive impact if you behave in either an aggressive or a passive manner.

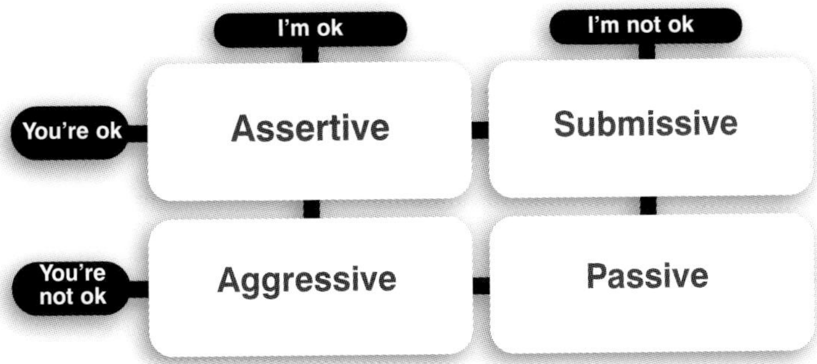

(Adapted from *The OK Corral,* F.H. Ernst, 1971)

ASSERTIVE BEHAVIOUR

Assertiveness is concerned with recognising your rights and those of other people. If people are behaving in an assertive manner they are generally seen as confident individuals who find it easy to earn the respect of others.

Assertiveness can be differentiated from aggressive and submissive behaviour through words, tone and body language.

	Assertive	**Aggressive**	**Submissive**
Verbal	Direct and clear – *I feel, I need*	Use of *I* in a threatening manner, using sarcasm	Apologetic, rambling, *if you wouldn't mind*
Tone	Steady, well-modulated, sincere and empathetic	Loud, clipped, hard	Quiet, muffled, tails off at the end
Facial	Open, good eye contact, interested	Glaring, staring, tense	Eyes lowered, apologetic smile
Posture	Relaxed and open	Strong gestures, finger pointing, leaning forward	Nervous movements, closed and shrinking

TIPS FOR BEING MORE ASSERTIVE

If you want to be more assertive in your behaviour the following tips will help:

- Always be confident, direct and clear when you speak
- Stick to the point and only include relevant information
- Retain a confident and open body posture
- State your expectations
- Label your emotions rather than just expressing them: *'I feel concerned that you are arriving late for work each day'*
- Use 'I' statements, but remember to respect the other person
- Be aware of your power base (refer to pages 38-39)
- Use positive self-talk (refer to pages 36-37)

It is quite easy unintentionally to move from assertiveness into aggressive or submissive behaviour. In order to make a positive impact, try always to be aware of your approach so that you can operate within an assertive frame.

NOTES

ACTION PLANNING

CREATING YOUR PLAN

An action plan is a way of breaking down a goal into small, manageable chunks or steps. At the very least, an action plan will help you define what the first step you need to take is… and that can often be the hardest part.

The basic structure of an action plan is as follows:

- Articulate what the goal is that you have set out to achieve. Make this specific rather than general
- Identify what you need to achieve the goal
- Construct a logical, ordered sequence of steps to get you from where you are now to the goal
- Work out how you will monitor your progress towards the goal
- Work out what might interrupt your progress/interfere with or sabotage your success
- Decide what rewards you will give yourself when you have achieved the goal

WAYS TO GET STARTED

1. **Start at the end and work backwards**
   Imagine that you are at the end of the process and that you have achieved your goal. Think back over the stages that you undertook and work out how you did it so successfully. You can take this a stage further by breaking it up on a timeline, starting at the end (with your specified time) and working backwards in units of time (that suit you) to see how you would go about achieving your goal.

2. **Brainstorming**
   Take a piece of paper and write your goal at the top of it. Fill in the answers to as many questions as you can think of that relate to your goal, and then plot the process that you need to take, based on your answers.

Make a contract with yourself – write it out properly. Put your contract somewhere prominent to remind you to stick with it when you are tempted not to.

The following pages provide you with ideas of where to start.

ACTION PLAN FOR INNER IMPACT

How you control your mood and your inner thinking processes will dictate the success of the action plan, so have one for your brain as well.

1. Get rid of irritations. For example, plan to deal with all the things in your life that distract you: leaking taps, poor coffee machine at work, not enough hanging space for clothes at home, etc. These minor points can take up so much mental space that focusing on yourself as a dynamic communicator becomes almost impossible. Resolve to tidy up the messy details of your life – streamline your brand.
2. Plan a way of dealing with stress. Start with finding out what triggers stress for you, when you feel it most, what aggravates it, what soothes it and plan strategies for handling chronic and acute attacks of stress.
3. Plan opportunities to use mental skills that optimise performance, eg visualisation, breathing techniques, etc. Put yourself in challenging situations and try them out.
4. Celebrate successes. No matter how small, if you have set yourself a goal and achieved it, reward yourself. This will motivate you towards bigger goals… and bigger rewards!
5. Develop an impact phrase to get you through challenging events where you feel vulnerable. Keep repeating this power-boosting phrase to yourself until you feel great.

ACTION PLAN FOR OUTER IMPACT

Sometimes, changing the way we look has the most unexpected impact on others, and their response to the change can create positive feelings of self-confidence in us.

When you have defined your brand, spend a little time thinking if all the choices you make represent your brand. If not, develop an action plan to bring your **self, projected** and **received** images all in line.

1. Go through your wardrobe and check for things you have not worn in the last year. These could be thrown away to make room for the *new you*.
2. Make an appointment to have your hair cut.
3. Weigh yourself, or measure your BMI and decide if it is appropriate for your height. If not, set up an action plan to shift a few pounds.
4. Be honest about how fit you are. Work out when and how to take some exercise.
5. Check your posture. Are you creating enough presence? If not, consider some sessions with a posture specialist and change the way others perceive you.
6. Make a decision to smile… often! This will increase your energy and have a positive impact on your mood.

FURTHER READING

BOOKS

Branding Yourself
By Mary Spillane. Published by Pan, 2000.

Uncommon Practice: People who deliver a great brand experience
Edited by Andy Milligan and Shaun Smith. Published by Pearson, 2002.

Develop your NLP Skills
By Andrew Bradbury. Published by Kogan Page, 2000.

The Brand You 50
By Tom Peters. Published by Random House, 1999.

The Relaxation & Stress Reduction Workbook
By Martha Davis et al. Published by New Harbinger, 2000.

Irresistibility
By Philippa Davies. Published by Hodder & Stoughton, 2000.

The Need for Words
By Patsy Rodenburg. Published by Methuen, 2001.

Taming Your Gremlin
By Richard D. Carson. Published by Harper Perennial, 1983.

Specialists

The Feldenkrais Method
Feldenkrais Guild UK Ltd
PO Box 370
London
N10 3XA

The Society of Teachers of the Alexander Technique
www.stat.org.uk

About the Authors

Pam Jones, BA, MBA

Pam is a Portfolio Director at Ashridge with responsibility for some of their leadership and performance management programmes. She works with managers to help them to understand and realise their potential and impact as leaders. Her expertise lies in the field of performance management, leadership, presentation skills, influencing skills and coaching. She is fully qualified in a range of psychometric instruments and is an NLP practitioner. She has written *Delivering Exceptional Performance* (Times Pitman, 1996) and *The Performance Management Pocketbook* (Management Pocketbooks,1999). She also has her own training and development consultancy, The Hiett Jones Partnership.

Pam can be contacted at: Pam@hiettjones.com Tel: 01525 221489
or at Ashridge on Pam.jones@ashridge.org.uk Tel: 01442 841092

A.J. Quinn, 2004

Janie van Hool, RADA dip, MA, MSc

Janie worked as an actress, prior to training as a voice coach and personal impact specialist. She is qualified in performance psychology and image consultancy, and has an extensive range of international clients. She works with managers and senior executives on a one-to-one and group basis, enabling them to enhance their personal presence and leadership impact. She is an associate of Ashridge Management College and contributes regularly on their open and tailored programmes.

Janie can be contacted at: 35A, Heathfield Road, Wandsworth Common,
London SW18 2PH Tel: 020 8871 1553 E-mail: janievh@aol.com

This book is based on Pam and Janie's work and research in performance, leadership, impact and impression management. They offer both one-to-one coaching and modular programmes.

ORDER FORM

Your details

Name ______________________

Position ______________________

Company ______________________

Address ______________________

____

____

Telephone ______________________

Fax ______________________

E-mail ______________________

VAT No. (EC companies) ______________________

Your Order Ref ______________________

Please send me:

			No. copies
The	Impact & Presence	Pocketbook	
The		Pocketbook	
The		Pocketbook	
The		Pocketbook	
The		Pocketbook	

Order by Post

MANAGEMENT POCKETBOOKS LTD

LAUREL HOUSE, STATION APPROACH, ALRESFORD,
HAMPSHIRE SO24 9JH UK

Order by Phone, Fax or Internet

Telephone: +44 (0)1962 735573
Facsimile: +44 (0)1962 733637
E-mail: sales@pocketbook.co.uk
Web: www.pocketbook.co.uk

MANAGEMENT POCKETBOOKS

Customers in USA should contact:
Stylus Publishing, LLC, 22883 Quicksilver Drive,
Sterling, VA 20166-2012
Telephone: 703 661 1581 or 800 232 0223
Facsimile: 703 661 1501 E-mail: styluspub@aol.com